# THE FLOOD, THE ARK, AND THE RAINBOW

By Stephanie Jeffs

Illustrated by Susan Wintringham

Abingdon Press

It was a dangerous place to live and everyone knew it.

The days had long gone since it was safe to walk through the olive groves or vineyards at any time of the day or night. You never knew who would be there, lurking in the shadows, waiting to steal your wine-skin or take your cloak. You couldn't even leave a goat tethered outside your home without watching it.

Arguments quickly turned into fights, parents with children, neighbor with neighbor. Gossip and lies spread quickly, and people dared trust no one.

It was a dangerous place to live, but it hadn't always been so. Only ten generations before it had been different. But the old men and women had forgotten the stories of neighbors helping each other, of brothers working together, of parents and children playing together.

Nobody remembered the time when the earth had been a garden and God had walked in it and had talked to the people God had created.

"This is a dangerous place to live," muttered an old man as he tried to get to sleep. "It wasn't like this when I was a boy." He propped himself up on his elbows. He thought of his own three children, who were now young men with wives of their own. What would the world be like when they were his age? Nobody was safe. Everyone was afraid but nobody cared. "What will happen?" he whispered into the night.

He closed his eyes. He felt a cool breeze brush over his face and then he lay down to sleep. He felt better now he had voiced his fears. He had not been talking to himself, or to the moon or the stars. He had been talking to God. He was the only man alive who still spoke to God. He was the only one who remembered God.

His name was Noah.

Daylight streamed through the opening which was Noah's window, and he sat bolt upright on his sleeping mat.

"A boat!" he exclaimed. "I have to build a boat!"

The sun shone its early morning light over the hills and trees. The world looked beautiful. Was he right? Had it just been a dream? He shivered and flung his cover round his shoulders. It had been an extraordinary night.

The last thing Noah had done before he had gone to sleep was talk to God. There was nothing unusual about that. He always did it. But what happened last night was unusual. Noah knew that God had spoken to him. God – the Creator of the Universe – had told Noah God's plans for the future.

God knew all about the people on earth – how badly they were behaving. God knew what a dangerous place the earth was. God had decided the evil and pain must come to an end, and had told Noah what was going to happen.

God told Noah that he was part of the plan to save the world. The job would take years to complete, and Noah was already an old man. But as Noah looked out of his window at the awakening world, he knew that he had to obey.

He shook off his cover, got up, opened the door and went outside. His wife stirred sleepily.

"I've got to build a boat," he said over his shoulder as he picked up his axe and set off towards the woods. "God's told me to build a boat."

His wife stared at the open doorway and shook her head. "What will we do with a boat?" she muttered. "We don't live anywhere near the sea!"

Noah carried his axe over his shoulder. He took some rope and his old donkey and headed towards the woods where the cypress trees grew. He did not notice the nods and glances as he walked past the well. He did not hear the whispered conversations or see the sneering faces. "I wonder what he's up to," hissed one to another. "Perhaps he's left his goat outside. . ."

It was hard work for an old man to chop down a cypress tree. It took Noah longer than he imagined. At last the tree crashed to the ground, and he sat on the broad trunk to rest. He wiped the sweat from his forehead and fanned his face with a leaf. It had taken nearly all morning to cut down one tree. Now he had to drag it home and cut it into planks. He had no idea how many trees he would need to cut to carry out the plans God had given him. Perhaps he was mistaken. Perhaps he had dreamed that he had heard God speaking to him.

Noah stood up. A gentle breeze rustled through the trees. No, he was not mistaken, God *had* told him to build a boat, an ark. God had given Noah detailed instructions. It was to be 135 metres long, 22 metres wide and 13 metres high. It was to have three decks, lots of rooms, a roof and one door. When it was finished he had to cover it in pitch to keep it water-tight. And then. . . and then. . .

"One thing at a time," said Noah to himself.

Noah lopped off the branches of the fallen tree and split the trunk in two. Using the rope, he tied the wood together and then tied the rope to the donkey. He gave her a gentle prod and she moved slowly forwards, pulling the heavy load.

"I think I'll ask the boys if they can help me tomorrow," he said to himself.

It did not take long for the rumor to spread that Noah had finally gone mad. By the time he returned home everyone was out waiting for him.

"Been fishing?" yelled a voice. Everyone laughed.

"What did you catch? A tree?" More laughter.

"I'm doing what God has asked me to," replied Noah.

The jeering crowd laughed. Noah tried to shout above the noise. "Listen to what God says. Remember the Lord God. God knows everything we think and everything we do. Don't forget God. . ."

By the time Noah returned home, his three sons were waiting for him.

"Are you all right, father?" asked Shem.

"We've heard some strange things about you," said Ham.

"And we're worried about you," continued Japheth.

Noah nodded, and looked kindly at his three sons. He broke off a piece of bread and ate it.

"I'm fine,"' he said. He ate some more and then he told them everything that God had said to him.

Noah told them that God had decided to destroy the earth, because the people had spoiled it. They had ignored God. They were cruel and selfish. God had seen the murders and the violence; he had heard the threats and the lies. Nothing that had been said or done, in secret or in the open, had gone unnoticed by God. God was going to flood the earth with water and destroy everything before it destroyed itself.

The three brothers sat in silence. They knew that their father prayed to God, and tried to live the way God wanted. They knew he wouldn't lie.

"What will happen to us?" whispered Shem. "We will all be drowned."

His father shook his head. "No," he said, and his eyes sparkled with tears. "No, not us! God has promised to spare me and my family. All of us! When I have built the ark we will go into it, and we will be safe."

"How powerful God is," said Ham.

The brothers left the house in silence. What they had heard was almost unbelievable, and yet they knew in their hearts it was true.

The next day Noah saddled his donkey and headed for the cypress trees, carrying his axe over his shoulder. He worked until nightfall and then came home, exhausted.

The following day Noah did the same. And the next day. Every day he worked on the boat, sawing and dragging the enormous pieces of cypress wood back to his house.

There were times when people came to make fun of him. They teased him and laughed at him.

"I am doing what God has told me to do," repeated Noah. He told them again about the Lord God who had made the world and everything in it. He told them that God had made a perfect world, but men and women had chosen to do the opposite of what God wanted and were selfish and destructive. Then he tried to warn them about the rains and the floods and the disaster which would come one day.

But nobody listened. It was too incredible to be true. There wasn't a cloud in the sky.

After a while people forgot all about Noah, just as they had forgotten all about God. They forgot to show their children the old man building a boat in the middle of dry land. Day after day they carried on lying and stealing, cheating and fighting. Day after day Noah worked on the boat. And by the time Noah had fitted the last planks of wood to the roof and covered them with pitch, the people did not even notice that it was finished.

From the very beginning, Noah had worried about what would happen when the boat was finished. He had not told his family everything about God's plan. Now he told them the next stage.

"Are you sure?" asked Ham.

"How are you going to get two of every kind of living creature to go with you into the boat?" questioned Shem.

"How are you going to feed them all?" wondered Japheth.

"We shall have everything we need," said Noah calmly. God had already instructed him to collect and store enough food for all of them.

That night Noah took a lamp and went inside the empty boat. He climbed up to the top deck and peered out onto the moonlit earth.

"Lord God," he said. "What shall I do next?" He felt the blowing of a gentle gust of wind. He stopped in one of the rooms and thoughts came clearly into his mind. "The family will live here, then the domestic animals can live here," he said as he moved from room to room. "We can use their eggs and milk." By the time Noah had reached the bottom of the boat he knew where each animal would live, and which rooms he would use to store food.

It was incredible to think that the boat was ready. As Noah looked at the finished boat, he knew that God would soon destroy the earth.

Once more he felt the cool evening breeze, and heard the unmistakable voice of God. "Now is the time," God whispered, "to take your family and all the animals into the boat."

"Tomorrow," Noah said to himself firmly, "tomorrow I will start collecting the animals."

Noah was worried about how he was going to round up two of every kind of living creature and lead them into a boat. God had also told him to take seven pairs of every animal which could be used as a sacrifice. Most of the animals were wild. Some were dangerous.

Sometimes Noah had lain awake at night and counted pairs of imaginary animals. He didn't even know most of their names! Building the boat had been a huge and difficult task. Now it was finished, Noah knew that somehow God would take care of the animals.

Early next morning, Noah noticed two goats following him as he dragged some bales of hay towards the boat. "Go home," he said, and pointed back to the way he had come. He walked on and after a few paces turned round. They were still there. "Who do you belong to?" Noah said, gently stroking the female goat's ears. She looked at him with trusting eyes. He walked on until he reached the ramp of the boat, then he led the goats into the room he had decided to use for domestic animals.

The first two animals were on the ark.

Over the next few days more animals arrived. They came to Noah as he gathered hay and straw. They found him as he went into the woods to collect nuts and berries. They slithered past him as he walked on the sandy heathland. They timidly approached him out of their secret hiding places. They flew past him and circled around him. They climbed up him and hung upon his cloak. They called to him from the plains, and they cried out to him in the darkness of the night. They sang to him in the early morning, and they slept by his feet as he counted sacks of grain. They came, trusting him.

Creatures of every kind made their way to the boat. Reptiles and insects hung from the walls and roof, and birds perched on ledges.

Noah did not need to look for them. They found him. They knew that he would keep them alive.

Noah was convinced that everyone would come from miles around to see all the animals. They would know that something extraordinary had happened and then they would believe that what Noah had told them was true. They would understand that God was going to destroy the earth. Then they would say they were sorry, and they would remember God.

But very few people came. Those that did grunted at the animals as if they had seen them all before. They looked at the cloudless, clear sky as if that was all the proof they needed. By the time Noah had told his family to go into the boat, he knew that the people would never listen.

"In seven days' time," said God, "it will rain for forty days and forty nights. I will flood the earth and destroy it."

Then God closed the door. Noah and his family waited. They waited for seven days.

Then it started to rain.

At first there was just a small grey cloud in the perfect blue sky. Then more clouds scudded together and fine drizzly rain began to fall. As the rain fell the sky turned darker and darker until it was completely grey. Then the rain fell with such force that it battered the earth. It ripped through the leaves and destroyed the crops. It pounded and crashed on everything.

Nothing could escape. There was no shelter. There was nowhere to hide.

As the rains fell there was a rumbling and a murmuring from deep within the earth. The rivers gushed over their banks in torrents. Springs of water exploded through the rocks and burst over the earth, so that the rivers and streams joined together with the lakes and seas. Before long the earth was completely engulfed in the thundering, swirling waters. Everything had been swallowed up, from the smallest insect to the highest mountain. Everything had been destroyed in the roaring unstoppable flood.

All that remained was Noah, and his family, and the creatures he had saved.

The boat floated, high above everything that had ever been created on earth. The wood creaked and groaned against the weight and pressure of the water outside.

As the days went by, the animals grew used to life inside the boat. All through the day and the night, the boat was filled with their activity. Although the boat was dark inside, with light from only one window, Noah knew when it was dawn. The male blackbird stretched, preened its feathers and broke into song. Pigeons and parrots, finches and pheasants all joined in, cooing, crowing and cackling. The wren sat up on its perch and started a piercing trill.

Then the other creatures started to wake, and the sound of birdsong gave way to other sounds, the shrill laugh of the hyena, the deep purr of the tiger and the loud screech of the gibbon. The porcupine and the panda woke with the puffin and the python. The skunk and the squirrel played with the stoat and the stick insect. The lions and leopards rested with the lemurs, and the elephants shuffled their feet beside the elephant shrew. As the bear fell asleep with the beaver, the bats awoke with the badgers.

There was a lot to do. Day after day, the animals needed feeding, and their living quarters had to be kept clean. Every human hand was needed. And as the rain continued to fall onto the boat, Noah and his family worked to create some sort of order, until they were exhausted.

After forty days and forty nights, the rain stopped.

Noah looked out, but all he could see was water. The boat had survived the bashing and pummelling of the rain. It had remained upright as the waters swelled and rose. They were safe. "Just as God promised," thought Noah.

The waters had stopped moving and churning. Noah felt again a gentle breeze. The breeze grew and the wind flicked up the surface of the water and slowly, invisibly at first, the waters began to drain away and evaporate.

The noise inside the boat was deafening compared with the unnatural stillness outside. Noah coaxed an inky black raven onto his hand. Then, raising his arm, Noah threw the bird high into the sky. The bird fluttered and circled above the boat until eventually it stretched its wings and flew off into the distance. Noah watched it until it disappeared beyond the horizon. He was just about to close the window when he saw a black dot in the clear blue sky. The raven had returned. He hadn't found land.

Days passed. Although Noah sensed that the waters were going down, he could not see any land. All he could feel was water, gently swaying and lapping against the boat. He sent the raven out again. Again the raven returned. Water still covered the earth.

Months passed. Noah's family and the animals on the boat could hardly remember what it was like to stand on firm, dry ground. Their bodies moved to the rhythm of the water. Noah looked at the raven once more and shook his head. He stuck out his hand and reached for a dove. He stroked the back of her head and gently ran his finger over her wings. Then he flung her outside the window. Like the raven, she flew out into the distance, and like the raven she flew back into Noah's outstretched hand. Water still covered the earth.

Patiently Noah waited another seven days and then he tried again. He watched the dove fly high into the sky until she vanished from his sight. "How much longer?" he whispered to the Lord God.

Evening came and Noah walked along the top deck. He reached to close the shutter on the window and as he did so he saw the flurry of white wings against the darkening sky. The dove had returned. Noah stretched out his arm and the dove lightly rested on his hand. In her beak she held a freshly picked olive leaf!

Noah shouted above the animal din, "The dove's come back! She's picked a new olive leaf. The waters are going down!"

For the next seven days Noah and his family took it in turns to watch the horizon. They felt sure that the boat was not moving quite as freely as it once had. It was resting on something, but it was impossible to see what it was. After another seven days Noah took the dove and tossed it into the air. Once again the bird flew away, glad to be free.

The dove did not return. Noah felt sure that this was a sign that it had found a place to rest. Then God spoke again to him.

"Noah! Now it is time for you and your family to leave the boat. Take all the animals with you. The earth is yours to enjoy. It is no longer a dangerous place to live."

Noah gathered his family around the doorway and opened the door of the boat. For a moment it creaked and groaned, and then the swollen cypress planks crashed to the ground.

Noah peered out and looked at the empty world. It was bright and new and clean. It shone in the light of the sun and Noah shielded his eyes from the glare. Then he walked down the ramp, his family and the animals following him.

They stretched their legs and bent down to touch the ground. It was completely dry.

"Look!" cried Noah.

His wife and children looked where Noah was pointing. The boat was resting on a mountain. From here they could see the valley below, with the pattern of the river, no longer flowing free, but contained within its banks.

They saw the woods and the trees, the rocks and the flowers. They watched as the zebra and lions ran to the distant plains and the fox and deer made for the woodland. They watched the snakes and lizards slither freely along the ground and the birds fly above it. They longed to run and walk with the animals. They wanted to explore the wonderful new world.

"Wait," said Noah to his family. "Remember God. Remember that God saved us."

Before he did anything else Noah built a fire and made a sacrifice to God. He thought back to the earth he had known and lived in, and thanked God for keeping his family safe. Tears ran down his face. "Thank you, Lord God," he repeated over and over again.

Then the Lord God spoke to Noah once more.

"Never again," God said. "I will never destroy the earth again. I promise that for as long as the earth remains there will always be summer and winter, night and day, cold and heat and seedtime and harvest."

Noah felt a warm breeze swirl about him and in the breeze he felt the word of God. "I will not forget you or your children. I have made a special promise to you which I will never break. Don't be afraid! The earth is yours to enjoy. I will give you a sign to remember my promise. Look!"

Noah would never forget what God had done, and neither would his children, he was certain of that. But Noah turned his face towards the sun and opened his eyes.

Across the sky was an arch of brilliant multi-colors which spanned the earth, stretching from one horizon to another. He gasped. It was wonderful. He had never seen anything like it before.

"This is my rainbow," said God. "I will write it across the sky so that you and your children and their children will remember the promise I have made to you today. Now go, and enjoy the earth."

"I will," said Noah as he stood up. He looked at his wife and his sons and daughters-in-law. He thought of all that they had to do. They had to build and plant and care for a new earth. He thought of the grandchildren he might live to see, and he smiled at the thought of them living on a new, safe earth. "I will enjoy the earth you have made," he said, as he reached for his cloak. "I promise!"

A Tamarind Book
Published in the United States of America by
Abingdon Press
201 Eighth Avenue South
P.O. Box 801
Nashville, TN 37202-801
U.S.A.

ISBN 0-687-09580-8

First edition 1998

Copyright © 1998 AD Publishing Services Ltd
Illustrations copyright © 1998 Susan Wintringham

Printed and bound in Spain